D0824578

WE THE PEOPLE

The Assassination of Abraham Lincoln

by Michael Burgan

Content Adviser: Tim Townsend, Lincoln Home
National Historic Site, Springfield, Illinois

Reading Adviser: Rosemary G. Palmer, Ph.D.,
Department of Literacy, College of Education,
Boise State University

COMPASS POINT BOOKS

MINNEAPOLIS, MINNESOTA

Compass Point Books
3109 West 50th Street, #115
Minneapolis, MN 55410

Visit Compass Point Books on the Internet at *www.compasspointbooks.com*
or e-mail your request to *custserv@compasspointbooks.com*

On the cover: John Wilkes Booth runs from Ford's Theatre after shooting President Lincoln.

Photographs ©: North Wind Picture Archives, cover, 4, 17, 27; Corbis, 5, 7, 11, 15, 18, 19, 20 (bottom), 32, 36; Library of Congress, 6, 12, 14, 16, 20 (top), 22, 23, 25, 29; Kean Collection/ Getty Images, 8; Hulton/Archive by Getty Images, 9, 13, 26, 28, 30, 35, 39; Taro Yamasaki/ Getty Images, 21; Edward Owen/Art Resource, N.Y., 24, 33; Bettmann/Corbis, 37; Tony Arruza/ Corbis, 38; Hans Wild/Time Life Pictures/Getty Images, 40.

Creative Director: Terri Foley
Managing Editor: Catherine Neitge
Photo Researcher: Marcie C. Spence
Designer/Page production: Bradfordesign, Inc./Jaime Martens
Cartographer: XNR Productions, Inc.

Library of Congress Cataloging-in-Publication Data
Burgan, Michael.
The assassination of Abraham Lincoln / by Michael Burgan.
p. cm. — (We the people)
Includes bibliographical references (p.) and index.
ISBN 0-7565-0678-6 (hardcover)
1. Lincoln, Abraham, 1809-1865—Assassination—Juvenile literature. [1. Lincoln, Abraham, 1809-1865—Assassination.] I. Title. II. We the people (Series) (Compass Point Books)
E457.5.B925 2004
973.7'092—dc22 200302417

TABLE OF CONTENTS

NOTE: *In this book, words that are defined in the glossary are in* **bold** *the first time they appear in the text.*

The Assassination of Abraham Lincoln • The Assassination of Abraham Linc

A Deadly Night

On the morning of April 10, 1865, 500 cannons boomed in Washington, D.C. Their firing celebrated an important victory in the Civil War. The day before, Robert E. Lee, the top general of the **Confederacy,** had surrendered to **Union** General Ulysses S. Grant. President Abraham Lincoln told Secretary of State William Seward, a member of his **cabinet,** "I think we are near the end at last."

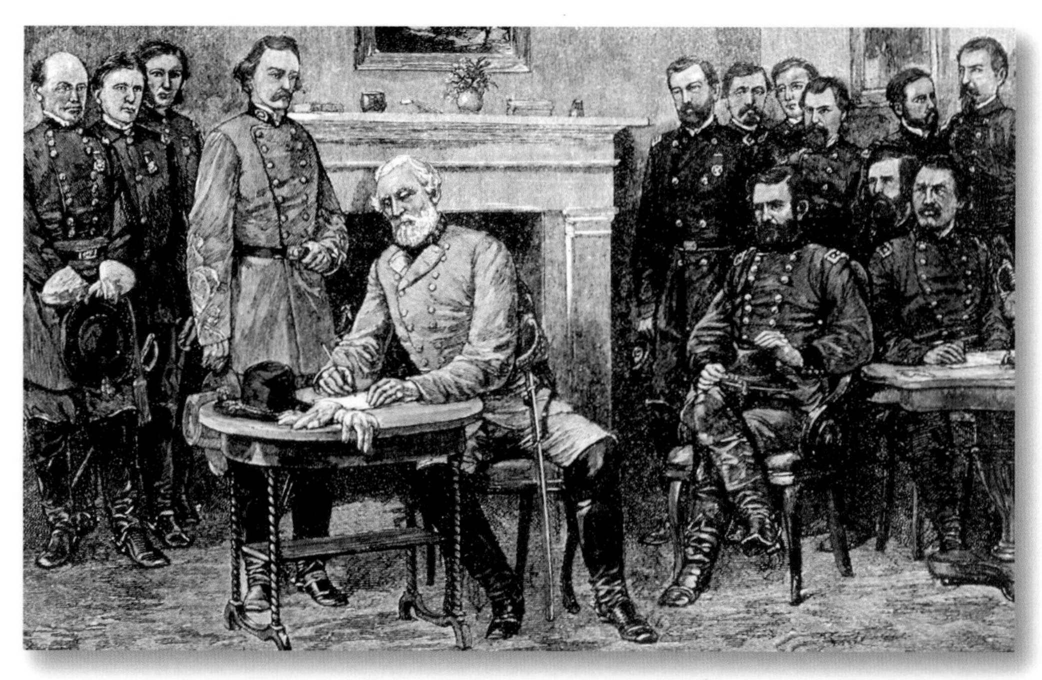

Confederate General Robert E. Lee surrenders to Union General Ulysses S. Grant.

President Lincoln visited the battlefield at Antietam during the Civil War.

For four years, Lincoln had tried to keep the United States together. A few months after Lincoln's election in November 1860, Southern states had begun to secede, or leave the Union. They then formed their own country, the Confederate States of America. The Southern states feared what Lincoln would do about slavery. Lincoln had often said that slavery was wrong and it should not be allowed in new states entering the Union. He did not, however, call for ending slavery where it already existed. Still, most Southerners believed Lincoln would try to wipe out slavery completely once he took office.

Abraham Lincoln meets with members of his cabinet for the first reading of the Emancipation Proclamation, which freed the slaves in the South.

The South believed its economy would collapse if slavery ended. Many Southern **plantations** and businesses used African-American slaves as their main workforce. Many Southerners also thought the U.S. government did not have the legal right to tell states they could not allow slavery. Seceding, the Southern states believed, was the only way to protect their rights and keep their slaves.

At first, Lincoln did not fight the Civil War to end slavery. He simply wanted to keep the country united. During the war, however, he freed the slaves in the South.

The Assassination of Abraham Lincoln • The Assassination of Abraham Lincoln

By February 1865, Congress had voted to end slavery everywhere in the United States.

After hearing the news of Lee's surrender, Lincoln knew he and the rest of the U.S. government still had plenty of work to do. Union troops had to defeat Confederate forces still fighting in several states. The government also had to find a peaceful way to bring the Southern states back into the Union and rebuild them. Many of their cities, railroads, and factories had been destroyed during the war. This rebuilding process was known as **Reconstruction.**

Many buildings and railroad tracks were destroyed in Atlanta, Georgia.

Assassin John Wilkes Booth sneaked into Lincoln's box at the theater.

On April 14, however, Lincoln took a break from his military and political concerns. He went to see a play at Ford's Theatre in Washington, D.C. At one point during the action, the crowd laughed and clapped at a joke told onstage. The noise masked the sound of a gunshot that rang out where the president sat. John Wilkes Booth, a supporter of the Confederacy, had sneaked into Lincoln's box and fired a single shot. That bullet killed the man who had kept the Union together—one of the greatest presidents in U.S. history.

Plots Against the President

With his views on slavery and his desire to keep the Union whole, Lincoln made many enemies, especially in the South. The threats against his life started even before he officially became president.

In February 1861, Lincoln left his hometown of Springfield, Illinois, for his **inauguration** in Washington, D.C.

In this 1865 drawing, the artist shows Lincoln riding near his house in Springfield.

Several people warned him that angry Southerners might try to kill him during the trip. William Seward wrote Lincoln that people in Washington feared the "possible disturbance and disorders" that might occur when Lincoln took the presidency. Most of the plots against him were just rumors, but Lincoln did face real danger in Baltimore, Maryland.

Maryland was a border state. It sat along the border between the Union and the new Confederacy. It was one of only four states that allowed slavery and still remained loyal to the Union. Yet many residents of Maryland opposed Lincoln and supported the Confederacy.

Allan Pinkerton, the head of a detective agency, learned about a plot to **assassinate** Lincoln when he reached Baltimore. Pinkerton convinced him to secretly change his plans and sneak into the city in the dead of night. Lincoln followed Pinkerton's advice and safely traveled by train through Baltimore to Washington.

Allan Pinkerton (left) with President Lincoln and General John A. McClernand

The Assassination of Abraham Lincoln • The Assassination of Abraham Lincoln

The Assassination of Abraham Linc • The Assassination of Abraham Lincoln

Once the Civil War began, some Confederate soldiers and citizens made plans to either kill or kidnap Lincoln. Confederate officials, however, rejected most of these ideas. One kidnapping plan was approved in 1864, but the general in charge of it was switched to another assignment, ending the effort. Another kidnapping plan that year failed.

Some Northerners also talked about getting rid of Lincoln. The Democrats were the main opponents of Lincoln and his Republican Party. When Lincoln won a second term as president in 1864, a few Democratic newspapers called for his assassination. A Wisconsin editor hoped "some bold hand will pierce his heart with a dagger point for the public good."

Abraham Lincoln

Booth and His Friends

The **conspiracy** that finally killed Lincoln began as another kidnapping plot. In 1864, John Wilkes Booth had contact with the Confederate secret service. This agency carried out the South's spy missions and was involved in at least one effort to kidnap Lincoln.

John Wilkes Booth

Booth, born in 1838, had grown up in Maryland. He shared the attitudes of many Southerners about slavery. He wrote that it "was one of the greatest blessings … that God ever bestowed upon a favored nation." Like many Southerners, he detested Abraham Lincoln.

Booth's father, Junius, and his brother Edwin were two of the most famous actors in the United States. John Wilkes was also a popular actor. His fame made it easy for him to travel through both the North and South during the Civil War. Booth had no trouble meeting with other Confederate supporters and making plans for the kidnapping.

Edwin Booth as Hamlet

The first meeting took place in September 1864 in Baltimore. Booth met with two old friends, Michael O'Laughlin and Samuel Arnold. Later, several other people joined the conspiracy. George Atzerodt, a German immigrant, would help the plotters cross the Potomac River once they kidnapped Lincoln. John Surratt knew people in Maryland who could help them escape. His mother, Mary Surratt, let Booth and his men meet at her inn in Maryland and at a small boardinghouse she ran in Washington. Also in the group were Lewis Powell (also known as Lewis Payne) and David Herold.

Members of the conspiracy

Dr. Samuel Mudd played a part as well by introducing Booth to a Confederate secret service agent.

Booth's original plan was to capture the president as he returned to the White House from the Soldiers' Home, a military complex just outside of Washington. Booth knew that Lincoln often made the trip with only a few soldiers

The Soldiers' Home was a military complex near Washington, D.C.

protecting him. Booth wanted to exchange the president for thousands of Southern prisoners of war. The conspirators also considered kidnapping the president as he attended a play at Ford's Theatre. The group decided this was too risky, and in March 1865 they plotted to kidnap Lincoln at a theater near the Soldiers' Home. That plan failed when Lincoln did not go to the theater.

Booth then decided to end the kidnapping plans. Instead, he and his assistants would kill the president. Lee's surrender to Grant fueled Booth's desire to kill Lincoln. The South was doomed to lose, Booth thought, unless he took action. He wrote, "Something decisive and great must be done."

Final Plans

On April 11, 1865, Abraham Lincoln spoke to the citizens of Washington about some of his plans for Reconstruction. Booth was in the crowd that night. He turned to Lewis Powell and said, "That is the last speech he will ever make."

By this time, Arnold and O'Laughlin had dropped out of the conspiracy. Surratt had gone on a trip to Canada, where many Confederate agents lived. Booth, Atzerodt, Powell, and Herold would carry out the assassination. For their final plan, they decided to kill Secretary of State William Seward and Vice President Andrew Johnson at the same time they murdered the president.

Lincoln gave his last speech at the White House.

Ford's Theatre in Washington, D.C., in the 1860s

Booth focused on killing Lincoln while he attended the theater. Booth knew people who worked at the main theaters in Washington. He would have no trouble learning when the president might see a play. Booth would also be able to get his friends in the theaters to help him.

On the morning of April 14, a Washington newspaper reported that Lincoln would be at Ford's Theatre that night. Through his own spies, Booth probably already knew the president planned to attend. He had certainly already visited the president's box at the theater and prepared for the assassination. Either he or one of his helpers had drilled a small hole in the door. Through the hole, Booth would be able to see Lincoln.

Booth also made sure the door to the box would not stay locked. Then, he hid a wooden bar he would use to keep the door shut once he entered the box. Finally, Booth kept a horse near the theater, so he could make a fast getaway.

The president's box at Ford's Theatre

The Assassination of Abraham Lincoln • The Assassination of Abraham Lincoln

The Assassination of Abraham Lincoln • The Assassination of Abraham Linc

April 14, 1865

On April 14, Lincoln met with his cabinet, as he usually did. He also saw several visitors. He and his wife, Mary Todd Lincoln, then prepared to go to Ford's Theatre. Going with them were Major Henry Rathbone and Clara Harris, the daughter of a U.S. senator from New York.

Mary Todd Lincoln

During the day, Lincoln had told his cabinet about a dream he had the night before. He was convinced the dream meant he was about to receive good news. That dream was much better than one the president had described to his wife and some friends earlier in the week. In that dream, he saw a dead body in

Abraham Lincoln

the White House, surrounded by crying people. In the dream, the president asked someone in the room who had died. The person told Lincoln, "The president. He was killed by an assassin." Lincoln tried to joke about the dream, noting that he was alive in it, while some other president was dead.

The Lincolns and their guests reached the theater at about 8:30 p.m. The show that night was a popular comedy called "Our American Cousin." Sometime during the play, Booth also entered the theater. A little after 10 P.M., Booth went to the president's box. Just one man stood outside it. Booth gave the man a card with his name on it. The man recognized the name of the well-known actor and let Booth into the box. Then, standing directly behind Lincoln, Booth fired a small pistol. The bullet struck Lincoln in the back of his head, and the president slumped in his chair.

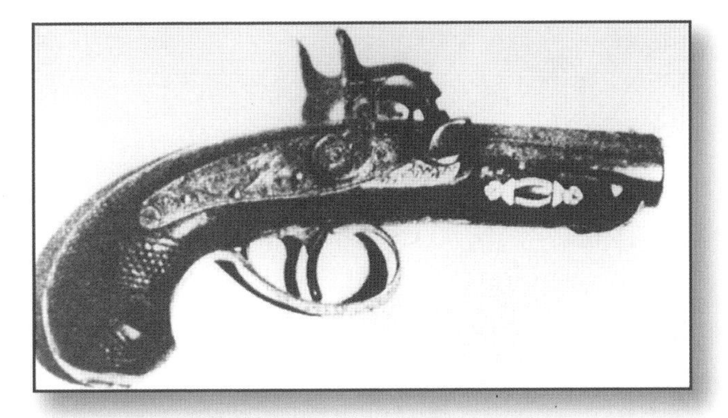

John Wilkes Booth's gun

In the box with the Lincolns were Henry Rathbone and Clara Harris.

Major Rathbone jumped from his seat and tried to tackle Booth. The assassin slashed at him with a long knife, causing a deep cut in his arm. Booth then leapt from the box to the stage. His leg, however, got caught on a flag hanging in front of the box. As he landed on the stage, Booth broke a bone in his lower leg. Then, just before hobbling off, he shouted *"Sic semper tyrannis!"* That Latin phrase means "Thus always to tyrants." By now, the audience knew something was terribly wrong. Mrs. Lincoln shouted, "They have shot the president!"

Meanwhile, in other parts of Washington, Booth's assistants were carrying out their part of the plan. Or at least one of them was. George Atzerodt was supposed to kill Vice President Johnson, but he lost his nerve and did not carry out the mission. Lewis Powell went to the home of Secretary Seward. Armed with a knife and a gun, Powell attacked Seward's guard, his son, and the secretary himself. A visitor to Seward's room later described seeing Seward "covered with blood, blood all around him and blood in the bed." All of the victims survived Lewis Powell's attack.

Secretary of State William Seward

Lincoln's Death

Back at Ford's Theatre, a doctor in the audience rushed to Lincoln's aid. When he saw the president, he thought he was dead. Lincoln, however, still had a faint pulse. A few men carried Lincoln out of the theater to a house across the street. They placed the president on a small bed. At 6 feet 4 inches (193 centimeters), Lincoln was too tall to lie straight on the bed. The men arranged him on an angle and placed extra pillows under his bloody head.

President Lincoln was carried out of Ford's Theatre to a house across the street.

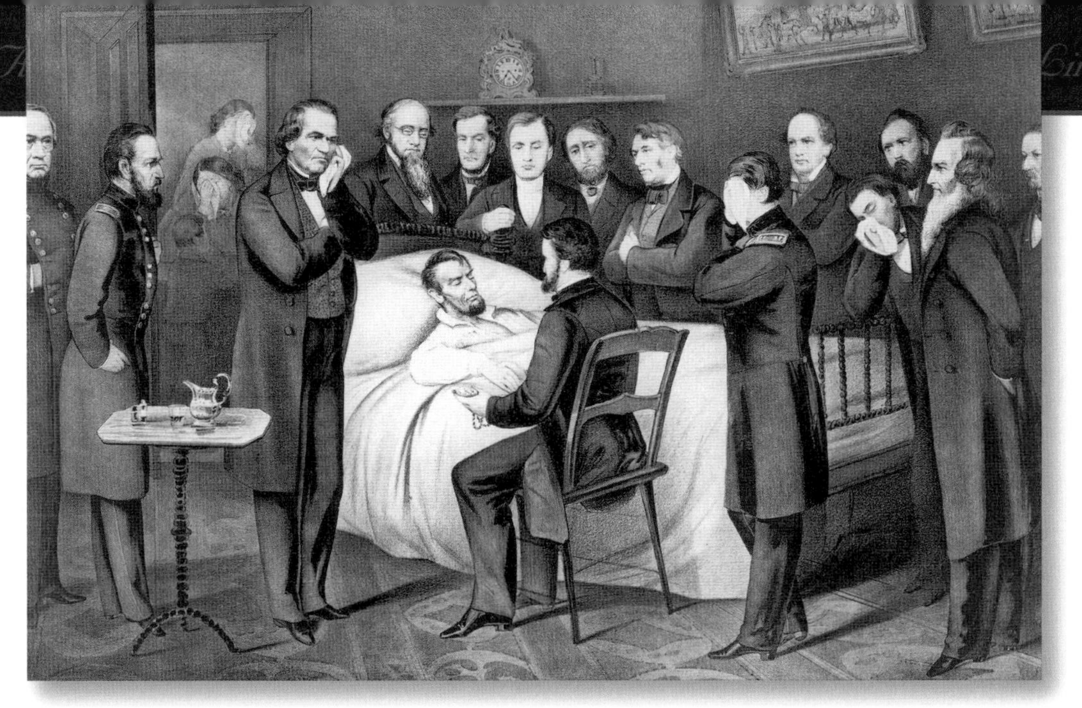

Artists at the time depicted a dying Lincoln surrounded by members of the government. In actuality, the men may have briefly visited the president, but Lincoln died in a tiny bedroom too small to hold all the people at once.

As members of Lincoln's cabinet heard about the assassination, they rushed to see him. By the time Secretary of the Navy Gideon Welles arrived, about six doctors were trying to save the president's life. Welles asked one how Lincoln was doing. "He replied that the President was dead to all intents, although he might live three hours or perhaps longer."

Slowly, Lincoln's right eye began to swell. His breathing weakened. Outside the house, concerned citizens gathered in the streets, waiting to hear news about their president. Inside, Mrs. Lincoln cried, knowing her husband was about to die. Welles wrote that he sat by the president's feet for several hours, "listening to the heavy groans, and witnessing the wasting life of a good and great man." Finally, at 7:22 A.M. on April 15, the doctors announced that President Abraham Lincoln was dead.

As Lincoln was dying, Secretary of War Edwin Stanton worked to keep the government running smoothly. He sent word to Andrew Johnson that he was about to become the 17th president of the United States. Stanton also ordered that bridges and roads leading out of Washington be closed, so the military could try to catch Booth and Powell.

Secretary of War Edwin Stanton

The Assassination of Abraham Lincoln • The Assassination of Abraham Lincoln

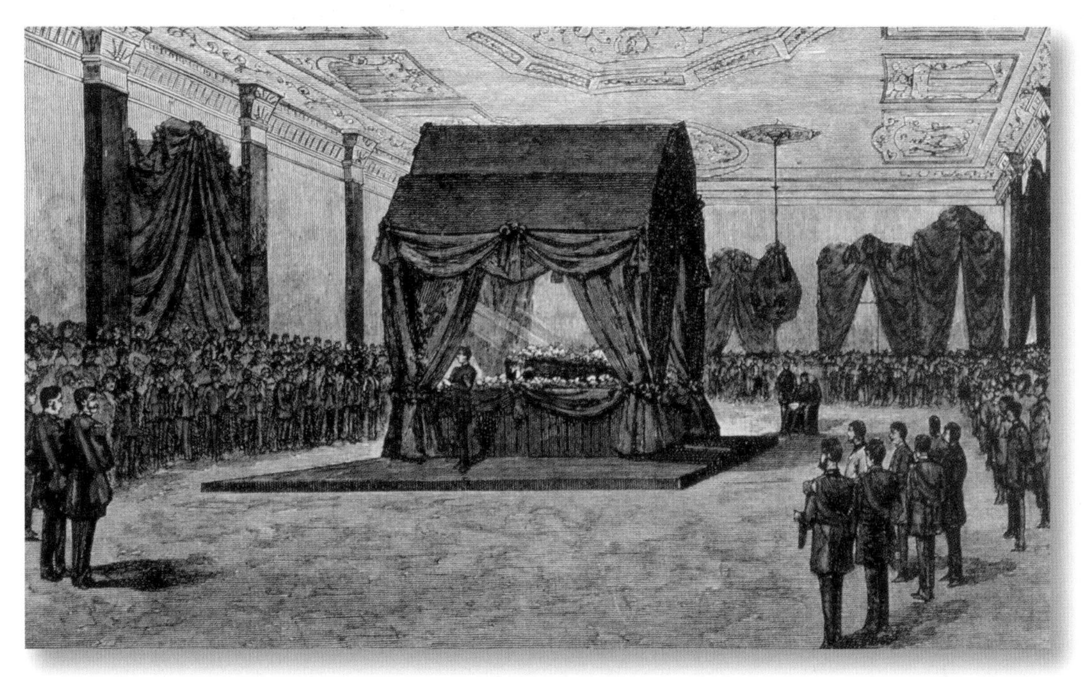

President Lincoln's casket was on view at the White House.

Word of the assassination soon spread, and the country began to mourn its fallen leader. Many people hung black ribbons or flags outside their homes. One newspaper noted that Americans "felt as men feel when they have lost their best earthly friend." The death especially saddened the nation's African-Americans. They deeply loved Lincoln for his efforts to end slavery.

Lincoln's casket sat for several days in the White House. Hundreds of government officials and ordinary citizens came to view his body one last time. On April 19, the casket was taken to the U.S. Capitol. Thousands of people lined the streets of Washington, crying as the casket passed them.

Two days later, Lincoln's body was placed on a train for the long trip back to Springfield, Illinois. The train stopped at several cities along the way, so more Americans could honor their fallen leader. Finally, Lincoln's casket reached his hometown, and the president was buried there on May 4, 1865.

Lincoln's funeral train stopped in Philadelphia, Pennsylvania, on its way to Illinois.

The Hunt for the Assassins

Government officials were determined to quickly catch Booth and everyone else in the murder conspiracy. The government offered a $50,000 reward for Booth and $25,000 rewards for the other main suspects, David Herold and John Surratt. Anyone who helped the wanted criminals faced arrest and **execution.**

A poster announces rewards for the conspirators.

After leaving the theater on April 14, Booth met Herold.

The two men rode to Mary Surratt's inn in southern Maryland. They picked up weapons and supplies, and then rode on to Dr. Samuel Mudd's house. The doctor treated Booth's broken leg. Booth and Herold then headed for Virginia, the closest Confederate state. By this time, John Surratt was in hiding in Canada, and he later traveled to several other countries to avoid arrest.

John Wilkes Booth fled on horseback, first to Maryland and then to Virginia.

A map of the United States in 1865 at the time President Lincoln was shot

Meanwhile, back in Washington, the police had found a letter that linked Samuel Arnold to the conspiracy. When questioned, he admitted that he knew about Booth's earlier plot to kidnap the president. The police also found

Lewis Powell in handcuffs

George Atzerodt, and he, too, confessed. From these two men, the police learned that Mary Surratt was involved in the conspiracy and that several other people may have played small roles. Michael O'Laughlin, the other early member of the conspiracy, turned himself in to the police.

The police caught Lewis Powell almost by accident. On April 17, several officers went to Mary Surratt's boardinghouse in the capital. Witnesses had reported seeing some suspicious men there after the assassination. As the police arrested Mrs. Surratt, a large man covered with dirt entered the house. Although the police did not know Powell was involved, they took him in for questioning. Seward's servant then recognized Powell as the man who had attacked Seward on April 14.

Booth was the main focus of the police hunt. For almost two weeks, Union troops chased him across Maryland and into Virginia. The soldiers knew Booth was injured, since they had questioned Dr. Mudd and found the assassin's boot at his house. The doctor then admitted he had treated Booth's broken leg. By April 25,

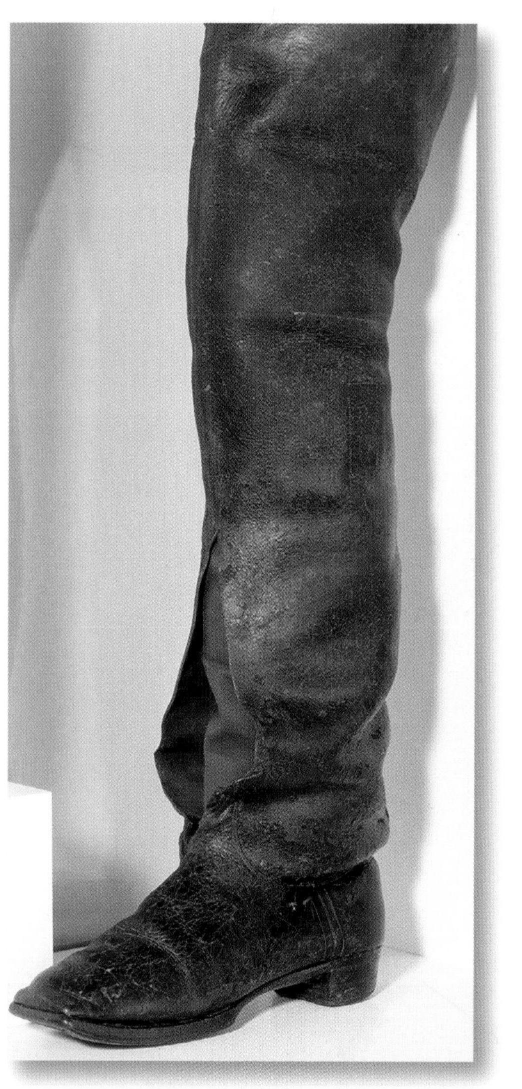

Booth's boot was found in Dr. Mudd's house.

the troops closed in on Booth and Herold as the two men hid in a barn on Richard Garrett's farm in northern Virginia. Booth wrote in his diary he had been "hunted like a dog through swamps [and] woods."

The Union soldiers received a tip about Booth's hiding place. After midnight on April 26, they surrounded the barn. Their orders were to capture Booth, not kill him, so he would go to trial. Booth, however, said he would fight to the death. Herold did not share his courage. He came out of the barn and surrendered. The Union forces then set the barn on fire, hoping to force out Booth.

The flames let the troops see Booth through cracks in the barn's walls. He held a gun in each hand. As Booth moved toward the barn door, perhaps to flee, one of the soldiers fired a shot. The bullet struck Booth in the neck. Some soldiers then rushed into the burning barn and pulled Booth out. He died several hours later.

Union soldiers dragged John Wilkes Booth from the burning barn.

The Assassination of Abraham Lincoln • The Assassination of Abraham Lincoln

Trial, Execution, and After

Northerners rejoiced when they heard Booth was dead. The rest of the conspirators, however, still faced a trial. A total of nine people were charged with being part of the plot. One of them, John Surratt, was still in hiding. The other eight were Powell, Herold, Mary Surratt, Atzerodt, Arnold, O'Laughlin, Mudd, and Edman Spangler, the man who helped Booth enter Ford's Theatre on April 14.

The government's case was the weakest against Mrs. Surratt. She had not played a direct role in the conspiracy. Still, on July 5, she and the others were found guilty. Mrs. Surratt, Herold, Powell, and

John Surratt

Four of the conspirators were hanged on July 7, 1865.

Atzerodt faced execution, which was carried out just two days later. One newspaper called the four "fiends" and said they deserved "that most dreadful of all penalties allowed by the civilized world—death by hanging." The other four

Fort Jefferson today is part of the Dry Tortugas National Park.

were sent to a government prison at Fort Jefferson in the Dry Tortugas off the coast of Florida.

The 1865 trial did not end the hunt for John Surratt. He was finally caught two years later. At his trial, the jury could not decide if Surratt was guilty, and he was freed. Two years later, President Andrew Johnson cut short the jail term of the other conspirators, and they were also freed. By this time, O'Laughlin had died in jail.

The Assassination of Abraham Lincoln • The Assassination of Abraham Lincoln

President Andrew Johnson

The assassination of Lincoln and the trial that followed has raised many questions. People have wondered who else took part in the plot. For a time, some Republicans claimed that Andrew Johnson was involved, so that he could become president. Few historians, however, believe this. Some do believe, however, that more people besides Booth and the others who went to trial played a role. Some historians also think the conspirators did not get a fair trial. Mary Surratt, in particular, probably should not have been executed. Others point out that she probably did know about the plot, even if she did not directly carry it out.

The house in which Lincoln died as seen from Ford's Theatre where he was shot

Abraham Lincoln's assassination came as the country was still trying to end the Civil War. Emotions against the Confederacy were strong. During Reconstruction, many Northern lawmakers wanted to punish the South as much as possible. President Johnson was not as strong a leader as Lincoln, and he argued often with Congress.

If he had lived, historians believe Lincoln would have had better relations with Congress and made Reconstruction easier on the South. Historians also think Lincoln probably would have done more to help freed African-Americans than Johnson did.

Lincoln's assassination forever changed the course of U.S. history. It also cut short the life of a great American.

Glossary

assassinate—to murder someone who is well known or important

cabinet—a president's group of advisers who are the heads of government departments

Confederacy—the Southern states that fought against the Northern states in the Civil War; also called the Confederate States of America

conspiracy—a plot among a group of people to commit a crime

execution—to put a person to death as punishment for a crime

inauguration—a ceremony at which a president is sworn into office

plantations—large farms in the South, usually worked by slaves

Reconstruction—the system for bringing the Southern states back into the United States after the Civil War

Union—the United States of America; also the Northern states that fought against the Southern states in the Civil War

Did You Know?

- Although Ford's Theatre is a national historic site, it is also a working theater. It features up to six productions a year.

- Mary Surratt was the first woman ever executed by the U.S. government.

- For many years, some people suggested that John Wilkes Booth escaped when he was surrounded by Union troops in Virginia. They claimed his body was not in the grave where he was said to be buried. In 1996, some of Booth's relatives wanted the body removed from the grave to see whose it was. Several courts, however, refused the request.

- Abraham Lincoln was the first U.S. president ever assassinated. The presidents assassinated after him were James Garfield (1881), William McKinley (1901), and John F. Kennedy (1963).

- The items in Lincoln's pocket when he died included a pocket knife and a $5 bill in Confederate money.

Important Dates

Timeline

1860	Abraham Lincoln is elected the 16th president of the United States.
1861	Seven Southern states form the Confederacy in February, with four more joining during the next few months; the Civil War begins in April.
1864	John Wilkes Booth begins his conspiracy to kidnap Abraham Lincoln in September; Lincoln wins his second term as president in November.
1865	Booth assassinates Lincoln at Ford's Theatre in April, while Lewis Powell attacks Secretary of State William Seward; Booth is killed in Virginia; eight conspirators in Lincoln's assassination are found guilty in July; four of them are executed.
1866	U.S. government buys Ford's Theatre; for the next 90 years, it serves as an office building, warehouse, and museum.
1867	John Surratt, the last known conspirator, is tried for his role in Lincoln's assassination. The jury cannot decide if he is guilty, and he is set free.
1869	President Andrew Johnson releases three of the conspirators from prison.
1968	A restored Ford's Theatre reopens with the play "John Brown's Body."

Important People

George Atzerodt (1835–1865)
One of the four people executed for plotting to kill Abraham Lincoln

John Wilkes Booth (1838–1865)
Well-known actor who assassinated Abraham Lincoln

David Herold (1842–1865)
One of the four people executed for plotting to kill Abraham Lincoln

Andrew Johnson (1808–1875)
Vice president who became president after Lincoln's death

Abraham Lincoln (1809–1865)
U.S. president who fought the Civil War to keep the Union together and who later ended slavery

Lewis Powell (1844–1865)
William Seward's attacker, he was one of the four people executed for plotting to kill Abraham Lincoln

William Seward (1801–1872)
Secretary of state who was attacked on the night of Lincoln's assassination

John Surratt (1844–1916)
Accused of taking part in the plot to kill Abraham Lincoln but never found guilty

Mary Surratt (1823–1865)
One of the four people executed for plotting to kill Abraham Lincoln

Want to Know More?

At the Library

Blashfield, Jean F. *Abraham Lincoln.* Minneapolis: Compass Point Books, 2002.

Marinelly, Deborah. *The Assassination of Abraham Lincoln.* New York: Rosen Publishing Group, 2002.

Otfinoski, Steven. *John Wilkes Booth and the Civil War.* Woodbridge, Conn.: Blackbirch Press, 1999.

Stanchak, John E. *Civil War.* New York: Dorling Kindersley Publishing, 2000.

Zeinert, Karen. *The Lincoln Murder Plot.* North Haven, Conn.: Linnet Books, 1999.

On the Web

For more information on *the assassination of Abraham Lincoln,* use FactHound to track down Web sites related to this book.

1. Go to *www.facthound.com*
2. Type in a search word related to this book or this book ID: 0756506786.
3. Click on the *Fetch It* button.

Your trusty FactHound will fetch the best Web sites for you!

On the Road

Ford's Theatre National Historic Site

511 10th Street N.W.

Washington, DC 20004

202/426-6924

To visit the site where President Lincoln was assassinated

Lincoln Memorial

23rd Street N.W.

Washington, DC 20037

202/426-6841

To see the national site that honors the 16th president

INDEX

About the Author

Michael Burgan is a freelance writer of books for children and adults. A history graduate of the University of Connecticut, he has written more than 60 fiction and nonfiction children's books for various publishers. For adult audiences, he has written news articles, essays, and plays. Michael Burgan is a recipient of an Educational Press Association of America award and belongs to the Society of Children's Book Writers and Illustrators.